The Spirit of False Judgment
Kathie Walters

Foreword by Dr. Larry Lea

Good News Fellowship Ministries
Rt. 28, Box 95D, Sleepy Creek Rd.
Macon, Georgia 31210

Unless otherwise noted, all scripture quotations are from the
New King James Version of the Bible.

To My Readers,

There has been a shadow over the Body of Christ for so long. We have seen a measure of the outpouring of the Holy Spirit, but it is nothing compared with what God desires to do. The Bible says that the "Whole of creation is anxiously longing to see the manifestation of the Sons of God" (Rom. 8:19). His glory will be seen as we forsake the things that dishonor Him and we learn not to judge and condemn one another, but to "Love one another fervently with a pure heart" (1 Pet. 1:22).

"Be kind to one another, tenderhearted, forgiving one another, even as God in Christ forgave you" (Eph. 4:32).

With Love in Jesus,
Kathie

Dedication

This book is dedicated firstly to the Body of Christ. I pray that it will bring understanding that will, in turn, produce love, forgiveness and unity.

Secondly it is dedicated to Arthur Burt, an old and very dear friend and "Father in the Lord." It was through Uncle Arthur that we first learned about judging (or not judging). God used him to bring great revelation of the ways of the Holy Spirit into our lives. Thank you, Arthur, for all of your faithfulness and patience to teach strong willed people like me.

Thirdly to my daughter, Faith, who suffers the indignities of my relating things like her "pink hair" episode to multitudes of people.

Two little children were eating ice-cream cones in an elevator.

In front of them stood a lady in a very expensive fur coat!

(Sister to little brother): "Be careful, Willie, you are getting fur all over your ice cream."

There is always another point of view!

(Borrowed from *Pebbles to Slay Goliath* by Arthur Burt)

Available from **Good News Publishers**
Rt. 28, Box 95D, Sleepy Creek Rd.
Macon, Georgia 31210

(912) 757-8071

Contents

Foreword

Dear Reader,

Learning the difference between false judgment which produces shame and death, and true spiritual conviction is the greatest challenge that we as believers will ever face. The Word clearly teaches us to hate sin, but never to judge sinners (or saints).

As I read through this most helpful material by Kathie Walters, I know that God will use it uniquely to give instruction between false judgments and true discernment and also to birth a new unity in the Body of Christ. With great courage Kathie has lifted her voice to defy the spirit of false judgment and accusation, and now is the time for that voice to be heard.

As never before the prayer of Jesus for unity is being pressed into the minds and hearts of God's true church. I challenge you not only to read this book, but to pray much as you read it, for it has the ability to direct your spirit and also to lead you into a new flow of grace and power.

Happy reading,
Larry Lea
Pastor, San Diego Lighthouse Church
8691 Echo Dr., La Mesa, CA 91944

"Lest Satan should take advantage of us; For we are not ignorant of his devices" (**2 Cor. 2:11**).

Preface

A number of years ago I came under attack from various people. Critical judgments were being made against me coupled with exaggerated stories and false rumors. At the time, my first reaction was to get angry and hit back. "Fight fire with fire." I thought I knew enough negative things about my attackers to equip me with plenty of ammunition. I was armed for a full-scale war, believing that the best form of defense is attack. In the midst of this the Lord spoke to me. "I do not want you to allow the nature of the wolf [old man] to dominate you, but the nature of the Lamb [new nature]." He then reminded me of Jesus, *"Who, when He was reviled, did not revile in return; when He suffered, He did not threaten, but committed Himself to Him who judges righteously"* **(1 Pet. 2:23).** *"He was oppressed and He was afflicted, yet **He opened not His mouth:** He was led as a lamb to the slaughter, and as a sheep before its shearers is silent, so He opened not His mouth"* **(Isa. 53:7).** It was not easy to keep silent, but the Holy Spirit enabled me. Sheep are helpless, not able to defend themselves. So they have to rely on the shepherd. When the wolves come to devour us, do we revert to the old wolf nature and bite back, or do we stay like the Lamb and allow the Great Shepherd of the sheep to vindicate us? No one is perfect. *"For all have sinned and fall short of the glory of God"* **(Rom. 3:23).**

Unless a person is in open rebellion and refuses to repent of their moral, ethical, or doctrinal errors, let us leave them in peace and pray for God's blessing upon them. None of us are qualified to make judgments. Only the Holy Spirit can know the motives of a man's heart. We often make judgments out of our own pride, forgetting that no one can stand except for the grace of God. It is His grace alone that keeps us from sin. We acknowledge the saving power of Christ, but often forget, we also need His **keeping** power. When a man falls into pride, God resists, His grace lifts and the man falls into the first hole (sin) that he comes to. *"...God resists the proud, but gives grace to the humble"* (**Jas. 4:6**).

Neither let us try to judge one another for what we consider to be "doctrinal error." None of us have, or walk in **all** truth. In fact, we are all in some degree of doctrinal error. Obviously, there are heresies, but they are to do with cardinal doctrines. I am referring to other issues that conflict with our own pet revelations or traditions. I believe that Kathie's book will enable you, the reader, to walk in a fresh relationship with God and with your brothers and sisters. She explains how to choose to listen to the Spirit and receive information from the tree of life (Jesus), and not from the tree of knowledge (natural realm) which is still forbidden (**Gen. 2:16**).

David Walters

Chapter One

Recognizing the Spirit of False Judgment

Isaiah prophesied of Jesus and said, *"The Spirit of the Lord shall **rest** upon Him, the Spirit of wisdom and understanding, the Spirit of counsel and might, the Spirit of knowledge and of the fear [or holy reverence] of the Lord"* **(Isa. 11:2).** For those who desire to walk in the Spirit, or to have the Spirit **rest** (or make His home) with them, then the scriptures here in Isaiah, chapter eleven, are the key to that walk and oneness with the Holy Spirit. Verse two describes the nature of the Spirit, and verse three describes the result of that relationship: *"His delight is in the fear of the Lord: and he shall not judge by the sight of His eyes, nor decide by the hearing of His ears; but with righteousness He shall judge the poor, and decide with equity [fairness] for the meek of the earth..."* **(Isa. 11:3).**

The Lord Jesus spoke of His ministry and said, "I can of myself do nothing. As I hear, I judge; and My judgment is righteous, because I do not seek my own will but the will of the Father who sent me" **(Jn. 5:30).** And again He warned,

1

"Do not judge according to <u>appearance,</u> but judge with righteous judgment" **(Jn. 7:24).**

Seeing Through God's Eyes

On one occasion, a good friend and father in the Lord, Arthur Burt, was staying in our home. On the bedside table, there was a photograph of a young man playing the piano. He had dark glasses and his hair was a little long. The picture was signed with the young man's name. It also stated that he was a Gospel singer. He had given us the picture a few weeks previously when he had come to minister in our church. Arthur had been for a walk and, upon his return, he asked me who the young man was in the picture. I informed him of the young man's identity and explained that he had recently sung at our church. "He is very anointed and he is blind," I told Arthur. Arthur frowned. Then he told me this:

> *When I was out walking, the Lord spoke to me and asked me this question, "What do you think of that young man you saw in the picture?"*
>
> *I replied, "Well, Lord, I guess it's just typical of this generation. These singers have to have some kind of gimmick, with the long hair and dark glasses."*
>
> *Arthur then screwed up his face, "I'm still learning not to judge after the outward appearance. You see, when I saw the dark glasses, I assumed it was a gimmick, but it turns out he's blind."*

How easy it is and how quick we are to make these judgments. How often they are **so** wrong. Unfortunately, many times we never find out.

Jesus did not make personal judgments of Himself (His own thoughts). He allowed the heart and mind of the Father to be revealed; and the Father, who knows the motives of the heart, made the judgments. The Apostle Paul states, *"But he who is spiritual judges all things..."* (**1 Cor. 2:15**). Well, who is he that is spiritual? Is it the one who has every doctrinal "I" dotted and every "T" crossed? No! It is the one who walks as the Son of God walked, dependent upon the Father, waiting to hear from heaven, not judging anything or anyone by the seeing of the eye, nor the hearing of the ear.

I believe that it is very important in the timing and plan of God that we, God's people, get some things straight. Many of us have walked in our own judgments for a long time, more out of ignorance than any evil intent. The Holy Spirit teaches us to truly operate our lives in the will of the Lord. That is our inheritance (**Phil. 2:5, Eph. 4:23, 1 Cor. 2:16**).

Commanded to Bless

Another very good reason for us to abstain from fleshly or ungodly judgments is because Satan would like to draw us into another spiritual realm in which we can be manipulated. If he can convince us to make judgments out of resentment or anger, or a critical and negative attitude, we will soon start hearing from an occult spirit. It will begin to tell us all kinds of things that are wrong with everyone. He will come and whisper to us, even give us negative visions and dreams about this or that person, or ministry. That spirit can begin to confirm and justify our negative feelings. He will make us feel that we are God's policemen to keep the Body of Christ in order.

I once heard someone say that God had called them to have a ministry of correction. What a deception! Have we ever taken time to stop and think of the grace that was given to us when we were at our worst? God has extended His grace toward us in the most glorious way. *"His love has no limits, **His grace has no measure,** His power has no boundaries known unto men. For out of His infinite riches in Jesus, He giveth and giveth and giveth again,"* as the old chorus says. If God has extended such grace toward us when we have never deserved it, how can we then withhold that same grace from someone else? We don't have that right.

We are commanded to bless like the prophet Balaam. He said, in response to a request by Balak to curse the children of Israel, *"Behold, I have received a command to bless; He has blessed, and I cannot reverse it"* **(Num. 23:20).** God's intent is always to bless. When the church is living in God's blessing and power, His name is glorified. If He brings correction, it is because His desire is to bless. If He brings judgment, it is because His desire is to bless and He deals with the things that are in the way. His love, grace, mercy, and power are to be demonstrated to the world, through the Church.

Ephesians, chapter two, declares that *"And raised us up together, and made us sit together in heavenly places in Christ Jesus. That in the ages to come He might shew the exceeding riches of His grace in His kindness **toward us** in Christ Jesus"* **(Eph. 2:6,7).** What a magnificent thought; God has set His affection on us. Why? To display to the world His great love, compassion, grace, and tender mercy. It is manifested in how He deals with us. We are to relate to each other in the same way and in the same Spirit. If everything we do is not a demonstration of God's grace, then we are acting against the work of the Holy Spirit. We are opposing Him in His ministry to the Body, and ultimately, through the Body. These are strong words I know, but God is not condemning us, He is wanting us to see through His eyes.

— Chapter Two —

Ready for God's Power

I was visiting with some good friends of mine in Orlando, Florida. I was in the home of Joy Strang and we were having a ladies' prayer/ministry meeting. I had a vision, which I believe was prophetic, not only for me, but for the Church as a whole. As we were worshipping the Lord, I asked Him what I should share with the women. He gave me, *"We were crucified with Christ"* **(Rom. 6:3-8).** The revelation of these scriptures had brought about a revival I was involved in years ago in England. Being crucified with Christ was not something we tried to accomplish, but a revelation from God that this was what Jesus did for us. By faith, as people saw that the old man **was** crucified, they were set free from many bondages. The spirit of joy fell and great manifestations of God's grace and power were present continually.

As I sat in Joy's meeting, the Holy Spirit came strongly upon me like a fire. It was on my head, my face, my arms, and my stomach. After a little while, it got so strong that I was unable to move my eyelids and open my eyes. I could not open my mouth, or lift my arms. I heard Joy introducing me, but I was unable to respond. I thought, "They must think I've fallen asleep." I asked the Lord what He was doing. Then I saw myself standing in some water about knee-deep. It was churning around my legs. I heard a great thundering, roaring noise and looked up. Right in front of me was Niagara Falls. I was actually in that water and I freaked out. It seemed as if physically I was being drawn toward the falls itself. On the inside I was trying to back away.

Then the Lord's voice spoke above the noise of the water,

> *"How would you like to get under **that** waterfall?"*
> *The thought was terrifying, yet at the same time exciting.*
> *"Oh no! I will die for sure," I replied.*
> *Then He said, "Not if you're dead already."*

My mind immediately went back to the scriptures I had been given in the beginning of the meeting. We **were** crucified with Christ, provision had been made. We did not have to come under the dictates of the flesh.

Spirits of religion and tradition cause great hindrances, because they deceive us into believing the wrong things. The sins and weights in our lives that need dealing with will be dealt with as we yield to the Spirit. He will lead, counsel, and cut away the dross. It is not by striving. Our religious flesh does not have the power to change the old nature. When Jesus died, He crucified not only our sins but the sin nature, the old man. That by faith we may walk in the new nature. When I had a revelation that Jesus did not die to change the old man, I was instantly delivered from several fleshy habits (smoking for one) **(Rom. 6:4-11)**. Religious striving brings great frustration, condemnation and discouragement.

7

Enter into God's rest by faith (read Hebrews, chapter four), and let the Spirit move in you both to will and to do of His good pleasure **(Phil. 2:13).**

I believe that this strong outpouring of God's power is on its way! God loves us so much that He wants everything out of the way. We then can flow in His power and bring deliverance with mighty signs and wonders to demonstrate His presence to our towns and cities. The power of God can be the most awesome thing we will ever experience on earth, but it can also be the most dreadful. It depends upon where we are and how we are living. If we are living in the flesh or in a religious, soulish realm, it can be devastating; for when real Holy Ghost power comes, sin is revealed.

In the early church the power of God was wonderful. There were miracles and healings and great numbers of people coming to salvation. But, the very same revival was crushing for Ananias and Sapphira **(Acts 5).** If we are ready, and are living and moving in the realm of the Spirit, and **learning to judge things according to the Holy Ghost,** then it will be the most glorious thing to look forward to. **(See Eph. 2:6)**

As the spirit of false judgment has operated in groups, churches, ministries, and individuals, it has kept us from the great outpouring of God. We have placed ourselves under judgment because of it. There must be understanding of what we have done, in that we have offended and grieved the Spirit of God in our making of wrong judgments. Repentance must come, and then the Holy Spirit will teach us how to move in the righteous judgments of the Lord. We will operate in the same mind as He. His compassion, love, and grace will flow.

Chapter Three

Avoiding Satan's Trap

A few years ago, my husband and I were ministering in New Orleans. The Sunday evening meeting was coming to a close. We ministered to individuals until 10:30 p.m. Just as we prayed for the last person, the Spirit of intercession fell upon me and also upon the pastor of the church. We only knew that it had something to do with "the church" in that area. We jumped into the pastor's car and he drove us downtown to two other churches. We sat outside and prayed for them, and also the many other churches in that city. Finally, the Holy Spirit showed us that there was a spirit of false judgment in the heavenlies. It had been released through the soulish judgment of a number of Christians. They had heard reports of one another from the news media and had judged accordingly without compassion, or understanding. The awful thing about it was that this spirit was now turning against the people who had operated in it. Jesus said, *"For with what judgment you judge, you will be judged; and with the measure you use, it will be measured back to you"* (**Mt. 7:2**). The spirit of false judgment operates when we make judgments and assessments without having the mind of Christ working in us. We judge according to what we see with our eyes, and hear with our ears.

Learning to Live in God's Judgments

As previously mentioned, we have a dear friend and father in the Lord. His name is Arthur Burt. He was a contemporary of Smith Wigglesworth, and has spent many years learning how to live and move in God's judgments, and not his own. He is a unique character, as anyone who knows him will tell you. I want to share some of the things that we have learned through this man. These lessons have not come only through his ministry, but also through my observation of his life and personal walk before the Lord.

Twenty years ago we were still living in England. During that time, we came to America on several ministry trips. On one occasion we had been invited to minister at a fellowship in Georgia. The fellowship consisted of 15-20 house groups which met twice a week. Each month they all came together for a large Sunday meeting. We knew most of the elders and pastors, but this time we were due to minister in a house fellowship that we had not been to before. The elder who was hosting us kindly invited us to go on Saturday evening and meet the leader of the group we were to minister with the next morning.

On this ministry trip, Sue, a young lady from our church fellowship in England, was traveling with us. She was helping and learning. When we got to the house, the leader came to the door to greet us. As I stretched out my hand to shake his, I saw a bold spirit of adultery looking right out of the man's eyes. It was so bold that I was stunned. We entered the home, and were introduced to several young men and the house group leader's wife. I was surprised to see Arthur Burt sitting in a chair, talking casually and drinking orange juice. He had decided to stop by and visit the church there.

Sue kept looking at me with wide open eyes. I knew she had seen the spirit of adultery in the leader also. As I sat and tried to join in the conversation, my thoughts were totally out of control. They went something like this, *"Well, Arthur Burt, I thought you were supposed to be a man of God. Surely, if I can see this situation, you can too. Why don't you* **do** *something? How can you just sit there and behave as though everything is O.K.?"* My thoughts continued to race around inside my head, *"Maybe Arthur can't see this thing. Maybe he's not as spiritual as I thought he was."* I couldn't understand it at all. Sue was still staring at me. I guess she was thinking the same thing about me as I was thinking of Arthur.

The evening wore on. Suddenly Arthur Burt put down his juice and gave out a very loud message in "tongues." Everyone nearly fell off their chairs with surprise at the sudden loud exhortation. It was like an explosion. When the message ceased, Arthur gave the interpretation. The message was all about having one more opportunity to put things right. In fact, it even talked about having until the next night. God would reveal after that. The room grew very silent and Arthur picked up his juice and resumed his conversation with another man.

We left shortly afterwards, and when I had an opportunity to be alone I asked the Lord about it. He told me this, "You see, Kathie, I couldn't use you because you already judged the man in your own heart." Arthur, in the natural realm had seen the spirit of adultery, but as far as he was concerned, he **didn't** see it, until the Holy Spirit revealed it. In other words, he was not influenced to do or even think anything, unless the Holy Spirit was saying it. The anointing came upon him and the Word of the Lord came forth into the situation. It was very specific. The culprit did not have to wonder what God meant. Arthur was completely detached from the word he gave, and he hadn't made a personal judgment as I had.

God alone is able to judge the motives of another person's heart. Always remember that God knows what He is doing. If He is after something in someone's life, He will speak privately to that person, sometimes repeatedly. He will speak directly and through His Word. Only after that does God reveal publicly, and bring judgment. Remember that the Holy Spirit is never negative, He always has a positive end in view — restoration. Neither is He vague. If you feel God is telling you to challenge someone about something, make sure that you are very specific, so that the other person is **not** left wondering what you were trying to say. I'm sure you would not discipline your own child without telling them why.

If you feel that the Lord has given you some discernment regarding a situation, don't hide behind someone and get them to say it for you. Be up front, don't hide behind anonymity.

Our ministry once had a prophecy letter signed, "Father." It was, of course, corrective in nature. I wondered who exactly this "father" was! Maybe it was Father Christmas. I don't think it was Father God. He always signs His name and says exactly what He means. I like how Roberts Liardon responds on such occasions, "Oh pleeease!"

We had some friends who were part of a church in East London. A visiting prophet came and ministered. The word he brought to the church was, "You are a rebellious people and you need to repent." The pastor asked the prophet in what way were the people rebellious. The visitor replied that he didn't know. Most of the people under the pastor's ministry had sense enough to put the word away from them, but other more immature ones fought a battle with condemnation for weeks, not understanding what they had done that was wrong. God never deals with His people like that. He brings a word of correction and the word brings true repentance which in turn produces life and healing.

People do things because of weakness and sin, but sometimes their heart is after the Lord. King David made a great mess with his adultery, lies, and even murder; but God referred to him as "A MAN AFTER MY OWN HEART." It's interesting to see that there is no record of Jesus being angry with sinners, but He was very angry with the Pharisees. The Pharisees made many judgments according to their **own** interpretation of the law and their own self-righteous mentality.

Remember though that, "Pride comes before a fall." When we get into pride, God resists and lifts His grace **(see Jas. 4:6)**, then we fall into the first hole that we come to. Because we are kept only by His power **(1 Pet. 1:5)**.

Chapter Four

Pink Hair!

I had a stunning experience recently. God really used it to point out something to me. I had been away for a couple of days, visiting and praying with Rose Weiner, a close friend of mine who lives in Gainesville, Florida. Rose and her husband, Bob, had a great ministry raising up churches on the campuses of the U.S. and in many other nations. They discipled and raised up many hundreds of young people, trained to take the Gospel to the nations.

My teenage daughter, Faith, had stayed home with a girlfriend to take care of our house and pets. Like any other parent, I had given many instructions about the care of the house, yard, animals, and pool. Faith is very sensible and capable, so I didn't worry about anything. I had called a few times and everything was fine. Returning home, I was not prepared for the shock that was awaiting me. As I turned the car into our driveway, the dogs came running to meet me as they usually did. I got out of the car and petted them, taking a second look at Faith's chow chow, Koa. He was usually a pretty, beige color, but his coat had turned to a shade of pink, at least down his back and tail. I wondered if he had fallen into a strawberry patch!

I entered the house, looking forward to seeing Faith, who being a home-schooler, was sure to be in the house. I went inside and began to ascend the stairs. There I was greeted by Faith who was standing at the top smiling demurely. I returned her smile, but my smile faded very quickly. Suddenly, I had seen it! A bright pink, wide streak down one side of her pretty blonde hair! Not a pale hint of color, but a peppermint pink!

"Faith, what has happened to you?" I cried. I thought there must have been some terrible mishap. She was joined by Haley, my secretary's daughter. Haley was grinning from ear to ear. Her dark hair was now deep green on one side and blue on the other! I freaked out! Faith laughed at my reaction — big mistake. I ranted and raved a while and she agreed to wash the pink out (dog too). A short while later, as I looked at her, I thought it didn't really look so bad. I let her keep it for a few days. I began to think about all this later **and** about my visit with Rose.

While I had been with Rose, another friend had called to tell her about a book he had recently read. It was offering the reader reasons as to why we are not in full-scale revival. Leaders who had made mistakes and had gotten offtrack here and there by overemphasizing various truths were named as being a major part of the cause for our lack. Rose and her husband had been mentioned in this book, along with other people that I knew well. I understand that the writer was concerned about the Body of Christ, but still I couldn't stop weeping whenever I thought about the "policeman" trying to get us all straight.

I couldn't stop thinking about Faith's hair, and my reaction to it. Her hair had gotten my attention and so my mind had to deal with what I **saw**. It took my attention away from all the things she had done over that weekend. It had been a hard job to look after the pool, because our area had been badly affected by floods and it was full of muddy water. Our house is a big house to clean, but it was neat and tidy. We have three phone lines with people calling all of the time. She had taken care of everyone. Our dog had been hit by a car a few days previously and needed a lot of attention. He was fine.

Not only had my things been well taken care of, but a family in her church had lost everything they owned in the flood. What was left of their house was under two inches of mud, and she had been over to help them clean. She had brought home three large bags of washing to do for them. She took care of the office. I had missed it all because of the pink hair. We can be so blind. Thank God for His endless grace and patience.

I then thought of the various books that had been written about the mistakes my friends and many other ministries had made at one time or another. They were obvious. Like the pink hair, most people could have seen them. But I thought, "What about all the thousands of young people who were saved and filled with the Spirit through their ministry on the campuses of America and many other nations? What about the thousands of kids who were dedicated to the call of God on their lives?" Thousands of young people received a very real sense of destiny in their lives because of the ministry and revelation of my friends who had given their lives for the Gospel. I wondered how it was that none of this was mentioned in these books. Maybe my daughter's hair is oversimplifying it, but it's the same principle to me.

When Rose told me about a very generous gift that had been given them for their China outreach, I felt so blessed myself. I wanted to write to the often maligned faith teacher that had given it and tell him, "You blessed **me** because you blessed my friends." When I heard about the negative things said in the book, I had a great desire to write and say, "You hurt **me** because you hurt my friends." I don't know of a ministry that has been around for any length of time that hasn't goofed at some point, said some dumb things from time to time, or headed off in a wrong direction occasionally. But, Jesus is the Great Shepherd; He will shepherd His sheep. He knows what He is doing.

It is the Holy Spirit who moves on God's people to convict and change. There is one thing more miserable than people trying to change themselves, and that is when we try to change each other. I can point out what is wrong with you, but **I don't have the power to change it.** When the Holy Spirit convicts, **He does** have the power to change it. Big difference!

Next time you are tempted to see only the obvious mistake in someone, say to yourself, "Pink hair." Maybe it will remind you that there are many wonderful things you have forgotten regarding that person or ministry. Jesus hasn't forgotten. He loves them so very much! We would put our hands over our mouths like Job, when God asked us, *"Where were you when I laid the foundations of the earth?"* **(Job 38:4)**, or, *"Were you there when I brought forth My Son from the grave? Were you there when I brought forth the firstfruits of THE CHURCH?"*

— *Chapter Five* —

Parents — Children

"Honor your father and mother: that it might go well with you and you may enjoy long life upon the earth" **(Eph. 6:2,3)**. This is the first commandment with a promise. If we obey the command to honor our parents, then we are promised the blessing of a long and good life. But, it presupposes that disobedience to the command will bring the reverse. To honor someone is to lift them higher than ourselves. We have judged our parents and in turn our own children have judged us. We have dishonored each other.

Do you remember Sue, the young lady I mentioned in chapter three? She had always had a problem in her relationship with her mother. To all intents and purposes the mother was not a great example of motherhood. She was divorced and had numerous boyfriends, thus making Sue's childhood very lonely. As a consequence, Sue had a hard time trying to live in the Spirit. She tried not to hate her mother. But she was bitter and cast many judgments on the parent. There always seemed to be a barrier to Sue completely entering into

19

the realm of the Spirit. As she was so tormented by this broken relationship, she spent quite a bit of time seeking the Lord.

The Lord suddenly showed her a vision of her mother's young adult life. Without going into details, it is enough to say that it was very traumatic and unhappy. This had led to a tremendous feeling of neglect and rejection. It had affected all her relationships, including those of her husband and child (Sue).

When the Holy Spirit revealed to Sue the inward state of her mother and the sadness in her life, it changed Sue's perspective totally. She was then able to repent from the wrong judgments she had made toward her mother. God gave her a compassion and new love for her. It was not too long before the relationship was on its way to becoming healed.

Children make judgments about parents today and there are many excuses for their anger given to them by psychological counselors. But there still has to be a repentance. Small children are capable of repenting when the Holy Spirit convicts them. We have seen many, many young children weeping and interceding, even repenting for nations, as well as themselves.

Just as we have had to repent of the attitudes and judgments that we have made toward our parents, our children in turn have to be taught that they do not know the reasons and inward parts of their parents' hearts.

Parents make mistakes, children don't understand the "why's," "where's" and "how's." False judgments are let loose like cannonballs, exploding in our minds and hearts because we have made the judgments without true understanding.

Chapter Six

Seeing the Body —
Through the Eyes of the Spirit

Years ago, when we first were baptized in the Holy Spirit, we heard a tape by Charles Simpson. I have never forgotten that teaching. It changed us. In part of it, Charles was talking about the Body of Christ and how we are all members one of another, and how we are to care for each other.

He said, "How many of you have gotten up in the middle of a cold night to go to the bathroom? As you were walking across the dark room, you stubbed your little toe on the bedpost. Ouch! That little toe was in **pain.** *Immediately your head sent a message to your right hand, 'Minister to left toe.' Your right hand went to the rescue immediately, held the toe tightly and caressed it. Then you prayed over it, and if it was hurt badly, you called the elders of the church to anoint it with oil. Why make all that fuss over a little ol' toe? Because it's* **your** *toe — that's why.*

"What do you think of this situation? Little toe gets stubbed on the bedpost. The head says, 'Right hand, minister to left toe,' and the right hand reacts like this: 'Well, I am tired of ministering to it, let someone else do it.' What if the right hand turned to the little hurting toe and said, 'I knew you were heading for disaster, I could see it coming. Now you're reaping the consequences and I hope you learn your lesson.'"

Does our own natural body behave like that? Of course not. But often our spiritual body does.

Let's be like the right hand who rushes to the rescue when the Lord gives the command. Sometimes we have to just be there. Maybe that's all we can do. It is only God who is able to sort out the messes and bring healing and sometimes that takes a little time. Meanwhile, don't judge. If the Lord gives you a word, that's great, but if He doesn't, your own observations will not bring deliverance, even if they are correct. Your heart has to be the same as God's heart for that person.

When my husband ministers to children, he often asks them the following question:

"What would you do if you saw a kid taking a hammer in one hand and hitting his thumb on the other hand? Wouldn't you think he was weird or crazy? Yet that is what we do, when we say or do mean things to others, whether it's our brothers or sisters, our friends, or even other church kids that we don't know."

The same principle applies to us as adults. When one member of the body attacks another member, we destroy ourselves. That's manifesting the wolf nature. *"For all the law*

22

is fulfilled in one word, even in this: You shall love your neigh-bor as yourself. But if ye bite and devour one another, be-ware lest you be consumed by one another" (**Gal. 5:14-15**).

Things Are Not as They Appear

When we were young Christians, sometimes we would visit another church or ministry where the Spirit was moving. It usually was great, because we never saw any of the problems. You have to live somewhere to really know what's going on. At the outset of the move of God in England years ago, there was a great movement of the Holy Spirit all over the country, especially in the South of England. In a small town, South Chard in Somerset, God was doing some great and extraordinary things. When we visited there we were overwhelmed. It was very powerful! There was an awesome presence of the Lord. People's lives were turned inside out and upside down in one meeting.

The people who were being used in that revival had paid a great price for the privilege. All that the visitors saw was **God moving in a mighty way**. But the people who actually moved location and joined that work weren't so sure when it came down to the "nitty-gritty." The daily hassles of getting along with each other were still a trial. Many people couldn't take it. It was hard on the flesh. But the visitors and the people who were ministered to never saw what was happening be-hind the scenes. They just saw the manifestations of a very gracious God who still made Himself known in the midst of a hungry people.

Most revivals come because of what we don't have, and not what we **do** have. There is a vast difference between yield-ing to the Holy Spirit and trying to earn revival or blessing.

True yielding is Spirit directed. Earning mentality is soul or flesh led. God is looking for hungry hearts. It is a fallacy to visit a place where there is a move of the Spirit and assume that everything is perfect, just because you are impressed or blessed. We all have clay feet. Some things appear great to your natural eyes and ears, but only God really knows.

I visited a church a few years ago where there was a lot of spiritual activity. From everything we heard and saw, it seemed like a spiritual utopia. The leaders were gracious and God appeared to be moving in unusual ways. It was very exciting. As we sat in the Sunday morning service, I spoke to the Lord: "I would just love to move here. This is where it's all **happening.**"

The Holy Spirit suddenly said, "No, you don't want to move here." At the same time, He gave me a vision and showed me that underneath the externals there was a spirit of pride. There was no way of knowing this in the natural, for the people were very sweet. They spoke about lifting up Jesus and the importance of having a spirit of humility.

A few years later, this same place was the very last place in America that I would have wanted to be. A lot of damage would have been done to our ministry. The work turned into a big mess. For our own good and the good of the Body of Christ, we must learn to hear from the Spirit and get our information from Him. We must learn not to be influenced by what we see and hear in the natural.

The Faith Message

There has been a lot of criticism of the "faith teachers" over the last few years. I have met people who have been alarmed and angry at the teaching of prosperity in particular. They assume that Kenneth Copeland, Jerry Seville, and others are out to amass a fortune by fleecing the sheep. If you don't listen properly, then I can see that it's possible to get that impression. But, whenever I have listened to these ministers, their prosperity teaching has always been in the context of financing the Gospel. It's easy to make a judgment after hearing a little about something. The Gospel is a Gospel of good news. Thank God there are people in the Body of Christ to get us delivered from our old, negative religious misconceptions.

One time, years ago, I fell and sprained my ankle. It was very painful. I prayed because someone told me that God was trying to change me, or teach me something through it. A lady in our church had come to my home and given me a Kenneth Copeland tape. I had made a point of not listening to it because I was sure he just wanted my money. God told me to listen to it and I did (gritting my teeth). God spoke to me and delivered me from that negative spirit. It changed a misconception that I had regarding the nature of my Heavenly Father. So much in my life was different after that tape. I repented over my very wrong judgment and guess what? Before the end of the tape my ankle was healed. On reflection I realized that nothing about my bruised ankle had changed me, it just made me irritable.

When we first began in our ministry, we really thought that because we now worked for the Lord, we would have to content ourselves with second-hand clothes and a broken-down car. No one had actually taught us that, but it was implied. Both David and I had good salaries and so it was hard to reconcile ourselves to having next to nothing. God intervened and challenged us by asking if we thought that He was not as good an employer as the people we had worked for previously. We did get delivered from a religious spirit and then we were able to receive from the Holy Spirit for our spiritual, physical, and financial needs. God wants us to be like water pipes, that can allow God's blessing, whether it be physical, spiritual, or financial, to flow through us. We are to prosper, but our prosperity is not for self-indulgence, but to glorify the Lord.

— Chapter Seven —

Judging According to Traditional Prejudice

Prejudice = To prejudge. To make up one's mind before hearing the other side of the matter. *"He who answers a matter before he hears it, it is folly and shame to him* (**Prov. 18:13**).

A famous evangelist once said, "Before you can convince me of error you must first demonstrate that you understand what I say."

On a radio program in our town a local church advertises. "Hello, I'm Pastor John Doe of the Misery Street Baptist Church. We are an old-fashioned, traditional, separatist church. We only preach from the 'King James' version of the Bible. We only sing the old-fashioned hymns. We don't believe in those modern songs and instruments, neither do we believe in using modern versions of the Bible. If you are looking for a church like ours, come and lift up the Lord Jesus with us next Sunday." Perhaps this pastor hasn't realized that the church did not begin with the "King James" version of the Bible. The organ and old traditional hymns were not used in the early church. Traditional prejudice has blinded many over the years. Most moves of God have opposed or even persecuted the next move of God that came. Men love their traditions more than they love the truth of God's Word. *"...You have made the commandment of God of no effect by your tradition"* (**Mt. 15:6**). *"And in vain they worship Me, teaching as doctrines the commandments of men"* (**Mt. 15:9**).

God is not only a creator but a God of variety. Blind tradition likes everyone to be the same and conform to its standards. It will often use ridiculous arguments to establish its position.

We were first filled with the Holy Spirit when we lived in England. At that time we were set free from a lot of traditional ideas which we had inherited from our evangelical foundations. After enjoying our new liberty for a while, we began to fall into the trap of establishing our own Charismatic traditions. We now believed in the moving of the Spirit! Rehearsal of music or sermons were looked upon by our church with suspicion. We sang choruses and preached messages spontaneously. People would "dance in the spirit" as they were led. It was all wonderful. As many young people started coming to our church we began singing a number of contemporary songs and have Christian folk music groups come in and minister to the youth. A little while later we found that other churches were using the "arts" in their church services. Ballet, choreographed dancing, mime and drama, were becoming popular. Initially we argued against it, but we were pre-judging according to our newly established traditions. Finally, we realized that God is not limited or obligated to our practices.

After coming to America, God stretched us a little more, for we had to accept a number of things that most traditional English Christians have a hard time with. Professional Christianity, such as the tele-evangelist and the showmanship that seemed to be a part of it, were very hard for us to understand. We had a real struggle to refrain from judging all of those people by what we saw with our eyes, but chose to believe that a number of them were motivated to glorify God.

When our daughter, Faith, was about twelve she started doing special worship dances in our meetings. Over the years she has not only continued to choreograph her own dances, but has other young teenagers join her. They now have added contemporary dances to music from the "Newsboys" and other groups that are popular with the teens.

A couple of years ago we heard a tape of a well-known Bible teacher. This person is well respected and held in high esteem by the churches that he is affiliated with. The message for the most part was foolishness, even though his hearers were shouting their approval. He was preaching against some of the new things that are happening in churches today. One of the points he made was that ballet or choreographed dancing was not of the spirit, but of the flesh. Although he admitted his daughter took ballet lessons, he said it was to improve her posture. He then went on to say that **(1)** Lucifer was in charge of the worship before he fell, so that proved that ballet was of the flesh. **(2)** If we close our eyes we cannot **see** the dance, and therefore cannot get blessed. Because of that, he reasoned, **it must** be soulish and not of the Spirit.

Taking that second argument alone, let's follow it through to its logical conclusion. He is using the concept of the senses. Christians are not to walk in the **sense** realm, but in the **spirit** realm. The problem is that there are five senses. Seeing is only one. There is also hearing. If, by closing our eyes we cannot see dancing, then by the same token, if we stop our ears we cannot hear the preaching. Does that mean that all preaching is in the flesh realm too? If only unrehearsed dancing is of the spirit, then does that mean that only sermons that have **not** been prepared are the only ones in the spirit? Does this also mean that singers and choirs should not practice their songs and musicians should not rehearse their music? Surely the question is not whether it's rehearsed or unrehearsed, but whether it is anointed! A person may jump up and begin to dance spontaneously in a church meeting. It could be in the flesh or it could be in the spirit. A person could do a special choreographed dance and it could be in the flesh or it could be in the spirit. Someone could jump up and sing in a meeting, it could be in the flesh or in the spirit. A person could rehearse a song and it could be in the flesh or in the spirit. A man could preach his prepared sermon and it could be in the flesh or in the spirit! The question is, is it anointed? That is the issue.

Religious, traditional prejudice always misses the point or is blinded to the real issue. Prejudice is so busy defending its position that it will not listen with an open mind to another alternative. The seeds of death are already in it, as it closes itself off to God's fresh revelation and creativity. If it continues in that mold, it will stagnate, decay and eventually die.

My husband, David, was speaking at a National Children's Pastors conference sometime ago and my daughter Faith and I were with him. We suggested that Faith could do a worship dance at one of the sessions during the praise and worship time. The organizers declined, feeling that it would not be appropriate, considering that there were over thirty different denominations present and some might be offended. We accepted that without question, but later in the week they had a number of children come in from a local church and do a rap song and dance to the whole assembly. It seemed that in their thinking this was no problem, but a serious worship dance might be. Was this illogical thinking and traditional prejudice combined?

David was doing some ministry in Tennessee last year and in one of the meetings a youth group came from another church. A couple of fourteen-year-old boys from the group looked and dressed in the weirdest way. One had all his hair shaved off except for one area on the side of his head where he had a long braided pigtail. The other had rings in his nose and both were wearing the strangest clothes! David had a struggle accepting their appearance. They definitely did not fit in to the typical church scene. He tried not to prejudge them. To his amazement, when it was time to preach they listened intently and drank in every word he said. When he prayed they were so gentle and receptive to the Holy Spirit that God's glory shone out of their faces. *"...For the Lord does not see as man sees; for man looks at the outward appearance, but the Lord looks at the heart"* **(1 Sam. 16:7).**

Bobby Conner, a prophetic minister, related a vision he had at a meeting in our town recently. The Lord showed him a vision/picture of a young man with purple hair and a ring in his nose. Bobby asked the Lord, "Who is this?" The Lord replied, "This is my new army." Some of us remember the revival among the hippies in California in the early seventies. Many of them were rejected by the traditional churches because they looked and behaved differently. Unfortunately some of the churches lost out and missed God because of their traditions. One of the reasons for the success of the Vineyard Churches has been because they have been willing to accept people that were not "respectable" or "churchy" looking. They have not made the mistake of making people conform to some kind of religious tradition. Of course there is the danger of cultivating a hippy tradition, where only that which is laid back, casual, and offbeat is accepted.

A good friend of ours has a great saying, "The anointing is pointing." Before judging what someone else is doing or the way they are doing it, let's wait and see if the Holy Spirit is anointing it. If we honestly listen to Him, He will let us know what is acceptable to God. We will all get some surprises sometimes, because we are all susceptible to prejudices.

Praying Against Principalities

There seems to be two schools of thought about this. One part of the church says that we are not commanded to take on this kind of warfare (praying against principalities). There are others who believe that this is partly what the church is about.

I believe that we should be led by the Spirit. God is doing some great things and if we walk with Him there are times when He gives the anointing to bind up those principalities. But to go ahead of the Spirit and simply decide to pray against those spirits can be dangerous. We have to walk with God and know His strategy.

In one place we were living, God revealed to us a spirit of false light and poverty over our area. The businesses failed and most people were really struggling financially and spiritually. It was very hard to get people saved, they didn't see the goodness of God (which leads to repentance). We bound that thing and threw it out (under the anointing). Within three years the area became very prosperous. Businesses moved in, nice subdivisions were built and people prospered and got saved. Several good churches arose there also.

Chapter Eight

Religious Spirit

Let me tell you about a friend of ours in England. His name was Mac, and he was a very likable young man. We had known him before we were filled with the Holy Spirit. He had been brought up in a Christian home, unlike the rest of us. We all envied him for that. He was a pleasant fellow. He actually knew his Bible better than most of us, because he had been learning from it all his life. We respected him greatly. He taught a class of new Christians every week and took special care of a couple of them. He met with them, prayed, and did Bible study. He faithfully gave of his time and energy. He was a real nice guy.

In contrast, David and I were involved with some rather worldly people. We were all Christians, but we were struggling because of our worldly concepts and life-styles. David and I both earned good salaries. Sometimes on Saturday we would get bored (a lot of Saturdays in England are boring because it rains so often), so we would sit down and try and think of things to go and buy for ourselves, or our posh little house in our posh little neighborhood! Our friends were mostly theater and television people. As a matter of fact, when I first met David, many of his girlfriends were movie actresses and chorus girls!

During this time, our philosophy was that you had to be like the world to win it. This was very convenient because it gave us an excuse not to change our life-style. We invited people to our elite little home, and offered them a cigarette and a glass of wine or whatever they drank, and then told them all about Jesus. Believe it or not, people actually got saved (kind of)! At least we tried!

Ironically, when we began seeking the Baptism of the Spirit, David and I got filled before our friends. Some of the people were very offended at that because of our worldliness. We were not considered to be very spiritual. They thought we didn't deserve for God to give us that kind of attention. What people didn't realize was that under the fleshly exterior we were **so hungry for GOD.** We just didn't have any power, and no one told us that we could have it. But God didn't go by the outward. He saw our hearts and met us in a wonderful way.

Meanwhile, Mac sat back and observed. He didn't seem to have that same hunger, but his wife did. He was not opposed and followed along with a kind of interest. Then a situation arose a few months after we were filled with the Spirit which caused us to realize how much we **assumed** things because of what we **saw** and **heard** in the natural. We were praying one evening for Mac's wife, Pauline, who was sick and losing the baby she was carrying. She was delivered from a spirit of infirmity. Mac came home from work during this time. While we were praying, the Holy Spirit suddenly gave me a vision. I spoke out the vision and my husband, David, had the interpretation. He turned toward Mac and said, "You cold, hard, religious spirit, come out of him." I thought David was crazy for saying such a thing, but Mac just slumped to the floor and lay still for about five minutes. Then he got up, a little shaken, but okay.

Do you know Mac never again came to any kind of Christian meeting? He was not saved. He said that the interpretation to the vision was correct. He knew about the Bible and he knew about Jesus, but he never did have a relationship with Him. He had a religious spirit from his upbringing, but he never had an encounter with God for himself. He didn't want too, either.

There are many nice, sweet people who would help out at the drop of a hat. That doesn't mean that they don't need to be born again. Some pets have nice natures, too. Our sin is that our lives are self-centered and not God-centered. We ALL need the blood of Jesus to cleanse us from that life-style. Nice or nasty is irrelevant. Hopefully, by now Mac has come back to find the Lord Jesus for himself.

We learned a lesson that day which we have never forgotten. You can't judge by what you see and hear. You must learn to listen to the Holy Spirit. He is the only one who really knows the depths and heights of **any** situation. God has such different views from our natural way of thinking. *"For as the heavens are higher than the earth, so are my ways higher than your ways, and my thoughts than your thoughts"* (**Isa. 55:9**).

I remember one time ministering to a very nice young lady. She was very quiet and unobtrusive, willing to help and serve. She had been under some bondage to a cultish group.

As I prayed for her, there appeared to be a hindrance. She was unable to receive deliverance. Suddenly some words just came into my mouth and I spoke out, "You have been stiff-necked and rebellious."

She looked at me with big, open eyes, and I felt awful as the tears ran down her cheeks.

"But, I've been so careful to try and be submissive," the young lady replied emotionally.

Inside I was praying, "Lord, why did You say that?"

Once again words tumbled out of my mouth, "Yes, but in your submission to man, you have rebelled against the things My Holy Spirit told you to do and say."

These were words that did not come from my thought process. God simply put them in my mouth. Sometimes supernatural "words of knowledge" and "words of wisdom" come like that. Sometimes they come in the form of a picture, and at other times, by scriptures. A lot of people have a very strong impression imprinted upon their minds.

Both the young lady and I had a revelation of what God was saying at the same time. She broke into a grin, as she saw what had happened, and repented. *The fear of man brings a snare [trap], but whoever trusts in the Lord shall be safe"* (Prov. 29:25).

To the natural eye, here was someone who had a quiet submissive spirit, but God does not look on things as we do. To obey something or someone else rather than Him, is sin and disobedience. But, it's possible to disobey **quietly**, in such a manner that no one knows what is going on inside.

Some of the most rebellious people I have ever met are religious, quiet, and sweetly stubborn people. Loud, noisy people are often thought of as being rebellious, but not necessarily so. God has created a variety of personalities. He wants to set us free from trying to be like someone else. Suppose all the jelly beans in the world were all green — how boring. Some people have very colorful personalities. That doesn't make them rebellious or "out of order." What has that to do with the heart?

Individual Accountability to God

When we stand before Jesus, we are going to be accountable. To say, "I wanted to obey You, but my wife wouldn't let me," or "I really wanted to go on in my spiritual life, but my church wanted to stay where they were," is not going to work. It's possible to disagree with someone, even a church, or stream or entire denomination, and not be rebellious. Have a good attitude and stay sweet in your spirit and in your heart. But we all have to do what we believe God is saying to us individually.

You Can't Judge by Appearance

Some years ago, I was involved in a street ministry to the prostitutes. I would go with others into the sleazy part of our city and talk, witness, and pray with them. Many of these girls were very open to the Gospel. A number came from Pentecostal homes. They had rebelled against the legalism surrounding them. We were very pleased that quite a few returned to their parents after we had prayed for them. God gave us words of knowledge which helped them know that God was real and that He knew all about them and their problems. They were very affected by the fact that God sent some-one to look for them.

One night, during our street ministry, I started talking to a tall, very attractive black girl. She was wearing tight clothes and was very carefully made up. We seemed to be having a reasonable conversation. She appeared amicable and fairly receptive, but I did feel a cold blockage, like an invisible barrier between us. As I was in the middle of a sentence, the Holy Spirit suddenly spoke to me. He said, "That's not a girl you're talking to, it's a man." My mind rolled over ten times and I gulped. Then I felt as if I wanted to throw up. He didn't give me anything else for this person. I knew the man didn't want to get into anything with me, and that was why he was being polite. I ended our conversation.

When someone is talking to me, I try and remember to listen to the Holy Spirit first, not the words coming from the person. Sometimes people don't even know what their own need really is. Like the woman at the well. She tried to have a religious discussion with Jesus, asking Him where He considered was the right place to worship. Was it in the mountains, or in Jerusalem? He ignored her question and told her what her problem was. She had five husbands and the man she was now living with was not her husband (**Jn. 4:18**). What had Jesus's statement to do with where she should worship? Nothing, but He cut through the outward and spoke to the inward. He was primarily listening to what the Father had to say about the woman, rather than to the woman herself. My, wouldn't we save a lot of time and needless talk if we operated like that? Of course we could lose a friend or two!

—Chapter Nine —

Supernatural Dreams and Visitations

There are many ministries in the Body who have been both written and gossiped about, especially those who have a strong anointing. They often draw attention because of it. It seems as though their mistakes always make the headlines. Any kind of revelatory giftings or experiences are held up to ridicule. They are the first to be brought before the firing squad. But their experiences have changed the lives of countless people through the ages. My daughter, Faith, was taken up into heaven when she was four years old. She spoke to Jesus and saw many things which she later described. A four-year-old's description may sound a little odd to some people. But she came back saved and filled with the Holy Spirit, speaking in tongues. She has served the Lord ever since. She is now seventeen.

I have had several dynamic angelic visitations, and two very special visitations from the Lord, the first lasting seven days. I was taken into heaven every day from 9 a.m. until 4 p.m. On another occasion, I was taken into heaven every day for three-and-a-half weeks. I can describe some of it to you, and I am writing a book about it. It may sound very strange to my evangelical friends. But I had such a revelation of my Lord Jesus! It broke the hardness in my heart. It caused me to be so in love with my Savior and gave me such an awesome understanding of the Fatherhood of God.

Roberts Liardon, founder of <u>Spirit Life Bible College</u> and <u>Roberts Liardon Ministries,</u> had an experience of heaven when he was a young boy. Read *I Saw Heaven* by Roberts Liardon. I have heard people mock his testimony. His experience is mystical, yes, but it still blesses thousands of people over twenty years later. Christian friend, if you have never had an experience of the Spirit yourself, you are not qualified to make a judgment about it. **I am talking about the supernatural experience that bears fruit for the Kingdom of God.** Many people don't believe in things just because they haven't personally experienced them. To quote Roberts:

> *"Spectators do not have the qualifications to comment on the participators. The guy who sits at home with a big bag of potato chips and a giant coke, with his feet up over the sofa, does not have the real ability to criticize the man who is running on the playing field from six, two-hundred-and-fifty pound, muscular, football player."*

People who have had the supernatural move of God in their lives and ministries have imparted to hundreds of thousands of men and women the revelation of a supernatural God, who is able to do for them **more than they could ever ask or think (Eph. 3:20).**

I Saw Heaven available — see "Books Available" list.

Chapter Ten

The Holy Spirit — The Encourager

Michele Buckingham (the daughter-in-law of the late Jamie Buckingham) and I were praying on the telephone one day. She and I have a common bond: we both have a deep desire for the Body of Christ to care, not condemn. We were asking God to help us see Jesus's Bride as He sees her.

I had a picture in my mind and it reminded me of an event in London years ago. God began to speak to me as He reminded me about it:

A young man that I knew was a competitive athlete and he had invited me to an athletic meeting in the White City Stadium in London. It was an international competition. I expected to be bored by the whole thing, but I found myself enjoying those athletes competing. I soon got into the swing of it and was caught up in all the enthusiasm.

The climax for most people was the last race, which was the mile. The runners were the best, and it had not been long since Roger Bannister ran the first four-minute mile.

The race started and off they went. It got more and more exciting as the runners gathered speed and the competition got tighter. Two more laps to go. Everyone was on their feet screaming and shouting. One of the runners was out front doing a good steady pace, and it seemed that he was a sure winner. He was a favorite. The excitement mounted. I found myself breathless. It was so exhilarating!

Suddenly, out of the blue, the guy in the lead tripped and fell hard. There was a gasp from the crowd as the disappointment shook the spectators. The runner was obviously hurt, but he struggled to his feet and continued in the race. He limped along. The crowd was so affected by his gallant attempt that they cheered and cheered. They weren't cheering now for him as **the** winner of the race. They couldn't care less. They were rooting for him as **"a winner."** The encouragement of the crowd gave strength to that man, and he ran well. Of course he didn't win, but in the eyes of the people he was the hero of the day.

The Bible talks about us running, as in a race (**see 1 Cor. 9:24).** If one of our favorite runners (ministers) falls, we often tend to cast him aside, because of his weakness. When that runner in the vision fell, he must have felt so discouraged, after all the weeks, months, and years of training. Imagine if those people in that stadium had yelled and screamed negative things as he made an effort to get back up. Can you imagine what would have happened if instead of cheers, he heard, "You missed it! You are not qualified anymore! Stay down! You can't run! You can't take part in this race!" Sentences screamed and thrown like rocks.

Too often our own runners (ministers) fall and they make no attempt to get up again. Others make courageous attempts amid the hostile atmosphere of the church. Wouldn't it be wonderful if the Body of Christ had that same encouraging tendency to cheer each other on? How many more people might make that finish line, having accomplished all that God wanted them to do, if their brothers and sisters in Christ rooted for them? Those outside the Kingdom would have a hard time resisting such **love.** Maybe that's what Jesus meant when He said, *"By **this** all will know that you are My disciples, if you have love for one another"* (**Jn. 13:35**).

When an irresponsible T.V. network did a critique of some ministries a couple of years ago, it did a lot of damage to the Body of Christ, but especially the people whom it zeroed in on. Larry Lea came under fire on that program. Facts were twisted to suit the concepts of the producers. Larry and his wife were not so much hurt personally by the program. After all, the T.V. world is looking for stories that will get ratings. They were more hurt by the fact that most of the Christians who saw the program just believed what they were told by the media. For most of the "brethren," there was no discernment, or taking time to get the mind of the Lord. The devil had a great time. He almost destroyed some valuable assets in the Church. Sometimes we are extremely *"...ignorant of his [Satan's] devices"* (**2 Cor. 2:11**).

Some other good friends of mine who have a very anointed ministry also came under some heavy enemy fire via the tabloids. One paper placed a photograph of their home in one of the sections. The picture was of a large, beautiful home, complete with swimming pool and tennis courts. It looked like a mansion. But the sides of the house had been extended in the picture so that it looked much wider than it actually was. The subdivision had a sports and activities center with a pool and tennis courts. The photographer had snapped the activities center and the paper altered the photograph and placed the tennis courts and pool next to the home of my friends! It was a deception. These things will happen more frequently as the spirit of Antichrist rises up. We have to learn to discern by the Holy Spirit.

False judgment can affect a whole church because the pastor comes under fire. As his motives are judged, he is "labeled" accordingly. Then his church, quite often, becomes a casualty as well. The religious Jezebel spirit attacks the move of the Spirit, the prophetic and anyone (including children) who begins to move out into the supernatural power of God.

The following pastor's testimony is a good example of this situation:

"For ten years I was part of a small network of churches emphasizing covenant relationships, which sprang out of the shepherding-discipleship movement of the 70's. For the last two years [1992-1994] my wife, myself, and our church body realized that the traditions and politics of our group were choking us spiritually, and hindering us from growing in God and discovering our identity in Christ. Our hearts were very hungry for the things of the Spirit.

"Although we discussed this with our overseers, we were gravely misunderstood. I was accused of pride, rebellion, independence, disloyalty and other sins. The leaders of the movement spent many hours on the telephone warning my sheep of my sin. We had to get an unlisted phone number because of the cruel and harassing messages left on our answering machine by one of the leaders.

"Needless to say, it was very hurtful to feel so betrayed, to be judged so harshly and accused so mercilessly, merely for desiring to go in a different direction. During this period of hearing slanderous reports, the Lord spoke to me and said that I was, 'not to return insult for insult.' By trusting God to vindicate me and refusing to enter into a war of words, the spiritual gale soon blew over.

"It was the most difficult experience that I have ever gone through, but the Lord helped us. Since that time the Lord has been graciously pouring out His life and blessing upon the church. God is prospering us, and people's lives are being radically changed by His power.

"I sincerely believe that in order for God to fully release His power in the way that He desires, the spirit of false judgment must be repented of. It tears and destroys. Its pride presumes upon the Grace of God. He only is the Righteous Judge."

Name available upon request.

— *Chapter Eleven* —

Acceptable Sins?

I was speaking at a ladies' retreat a while ago. The Lord had given me a picture and a word. He said that to be ready for the outpouring of the Spirit, we must allow His heart for others to be manifested in each of us. He showed me a room that was dusty and disorderly. Suddenly Jesus came into the room and began to clean it up. He dusted the cobwebs, and swept it out. He rearranged the furniture (doctrines) and threw some of it out. Then He took up residence; it became His room. The room represented our hearts and minds. He will not do this if we are determined to hang on to our religious and pharisaical ways. But if we are willing to allow Him to come in, then He will change our minds and hearts about things which presently hinder us.

Can you imagine a friend inviting you to spend a few weeks at their home? When you arrived they invited you inside and said, "Find yourself somewhere to sleep," nodding toward the sofa. "There is some food in the fridge. I have some things to do, I'll be back later." What if, for the

46

next few days, they just continued on with their lives as though you weren't there? Would you not very soon find an excuse to leave? Wouldn't you feel very uncomfortable and unwelcome? Of course you would!

Well, the Holy Spirit must feel like that sometimes. We invite Him to come in and be a very welcome guest, but after a while we get busy doing our own thing and leave Him out (except for Sunday morning). We don't seem to think of that as sin, but it is. It is separating ourselves because of our independent spirit.

Isn't it a shame that in our religious minds we make some sins acceptable and some unacceptable? Any moral kind of sin is somehow **unforgivable.** But anger, resentment, bitterness, criticism, gossip, slander, etc., doesn't seem so bad to our natural mind.

Bitterness, for example, has a far-reaching effect upon those it touches. It has the ability to contaminate others, as well as the person who has it. Scripture tells us, *"Looking carefully lest any one fall short of the grace of God; lest any root of bitterness springing up cause trouble, and by this many become defiled"* (**Heb. 12:15**). I have known many people who have kept their bitterness for years. It has come forth from their mouths like poison, a continual stream, defiling hundreds of other Christians. Why do I not hear that self-righteous cry for them to be taken out of the ministry, out of their pulpits, etc.? It's because somehow their sin is not so offensive to the rest of us as someone who falls into adultery. Even though the adultery, for example, may have been a one-time incident, the remembrance of it follows them for years. Whenever they get up and get going again it shouts indignantly and throws accusations like stones. What a sorry state we are in, so full of dead men's bones and religious adages.

I was so sorry to hear recently about the fall of a popular Christian singer. I know that in spite of his repentance, and regret, it will probably finish his career in Christian music. I heard of his tapes, etc., being withdrawn from many of the Christian bookstores. I was sad, not just because he fell, but because I wondered if the rest of us would ever let him get up and continue on.

I have prayed for many, many people who have had things in their past of which they are ashamed. Most of us would not want our Christian brothers and sisters to really know what we were like before we were born again. Praise God for the *"...Blood of Jesus Christ His Son cleanses us from all sin"* **(1 Jn. 1:7).** But I have cast out the spirit of shame from many Christians who have had failures during their spiritual walk. Although they have known they were forgiven, the feeling of condemnation, shame and guilt was still present. Those things are spirits and have to be prayed against. This is another reason that we have to be so careful about our judgments. Our self-righteous attitude can keep people bound in shame for a long time.

If someone has repented of their sin, God has put it away. *"As far as the east is from the west, so far has He removed our transgressions from us"* **(Ps. 103:12).** I once heard a discussion about a brother who had fallen into sin. I couldn't believe it when one of the pastors stated that he didn't believe the brother had repented properly. "PROPERLY — WHAT DOES THAT MEAN?" I thought to myself. I was so angry that I did not dare say a word. Who do we think we are? How do we know if someone has repented "properly"?

That's scary! Sometimes we play God. Remember those un-just judgments are coming back to us. *"...For with the same measure that you use, it will be measured back to you"* **(Lk. 6:36-38).** Jesus was talking about two things...judging in v. 36,37 and giving in v. 38.

Have you ever considered tossing away message tapes or books because you heard something negative? Maybe we all had better cut out the Psalms of David from our Bibles. Could we possibly be blessed by so great a sinner as King David? I read a passage of scripture that seemed God had designed especially to blow our religious little minds. In the first book of Kings the prophet Ahijah gives the wife of Jeroboam a message for Jeroboam from the Lord. He says, *"...And yet you have not been as my servant David, who kept my com-mandments and followed me **with all his heart,** to do only what was right in My eyes"* **(1 Kgs. 14:8).** As previously mentioned, not only did David commit adultery, he lied, cheated, schemed, manipulated, and made sure Uriah, Bathsheba's husband, was killed. Uriah was in the way of King David's lustful plan. The way he disposed of his prob-lem was a bit extreme (he did not just fire Uriah from his position). But God continually referred to David as a man after His own heart and always referred to him as, "My ser-vant."

Arthur Burt once told us how many people have a prob-lem with receiving from people they consider not up to their spiritual par. "How can God speak through that man? There are so many things wrong with his life." If the mailman de-livers us a letter, do we refuse to accept it because he is wear-ing dirty boots? God will use whomever He chooses. Some-times He sends someone we have a problem with in order to humble us. I wonder how many times we have all missed something from God? Perhaps it was because we weren't really open to someone we considered less spiritual than ourselves, or were not part of our denomination or religious stream.

Maybe those of us in full time ministry should reassess some of our own values. I have witnessed, more times than I care to count, God's "anointed" vessels behaving as though they were the only important saints in the kingdom. Throwing their weight around and talking to the people and staff around and about them as if their only calling in life was to be their servants. Rudeness is not necessary. Bad manners are ungracious, ungodly and ugly. Even the quietest, smallest child of God should be respected and encouraged. Jesus died for each one and He lovingly and passionately cares for every living stone. Each one is going to shine forth as gold. It takes **all** of us to make His temple complete.

There is a religious, legalistic spirit that demands that we somehow "qualify" to be used by God. Again, there are some sins that seem to be acceptable and some unacceptable. I have heard some teachers say that if someone has been divorced there is no longer any room for them in the ministry, although they have been forgiven. Granted, if a man or woman makes a habit of discarding a mate, they would probably do that to the sheep as well, and I would be cautious. Every person in the ministry that I know personally who has been in a divorce has been in that place because of ignorance, unbelief or because of an irrevocable situation. Jesus told the pharisees that He wanted mercy, and not sacrifice **(Mt. 12:7).** If we judge others by the law, we will also be judged by the law.

— *Chapter Twelve* —

The Button

At a prayer meeting in Atlanta recently, the intercessors were praying for a friend of mine who has a powerful ministry. This man is a strong Christian, not easily discouraged. A fighter. But I had talked to him on the telephone the previous day and I had never heard him sound so down and discouraged. I was going to relate some of his spiritual exploits in another book of mine. He seemed fearful that if I honored him in any way, it would just remind all the professional critics of his past failures and give them another opportunity to attack his ministry. We began to pray and intercede.

The Holy Spirit gave me a vision. The picture I saw was of some brothers going into this minister's home. He had invited them into his house because he trusted them. The brothers arrived early and my friend still had on his pajamas. Because they were good friends he opened the door, even though he wasn't dressed to receive them. My friend had a button missing from his pajama jacket. One of those visiting brothers noticed the missing button and pointed to it. He then ran out into the street calling out to others about the missing button. It reminded me of Ham **(Gen. 9:22-25),** who saw his father's (Noah) nakedness and ran and told his two brothers. A curse came upon Canaan, Ham's son, because of his tale-telling. That account alone should be enough to make us think twice before repeating things we see and hear.

Thinking again of the button, a friend, truly concerned, would get some thread and a needle and help sew the button back on. The man was hurt by the reaction of the other men.

I am not saying that it doesn't matter at all about the hurts and wounds that are caused by mistakes that are made by people in the ministry. As much as is possible they should put things right, but still we are not to judge. The way to deal with those things is by covering and caring, not by exposing. The Holy Spirit will do any exposing that needs to be done. He doesn't need us to run into the street with the news.

As regards personal hurts and wounds, we individually have a responsibility to get healed. God has made many promises in His word with regard to healing, emotional and physical. In my experience, healing is linked to forgiveness. We have to forgive and then healing will come. Forgiveness is not a feeling, it's an act we make by faith. Don't afterwards let the devil tempt you to receive those negative feelings of unforgiveness back again.

Sometimes when a heartache, hurt, or grief has been around a while, it can take up residence inside. I often pray for people at women's conferences and retreats to be delivered from those things. I take authority over them in the name of Jesus, and command them to leave.

God does not want us walking around with all kinds of "diseases" in our hearts. Resentment, unforgiveness, anger, bitterness, etc., quench the abiding presence of the Holy Spirit in our lives. We can take control over those things and refuse them. I tell people I minister to, "The devil is not really that interested in you personally, he doesn't care what happens to you. He doesn't care if you go to Bible study six times a week. His only concern is to get you out of the Spirit, or out of the anointing. Whatever it takes to get each one out of the spirit-walk, is what Satan will do. With one person it may be anger, or fear, with another frustration. He knows our weaknesses, he knows what will get YOU out of the anointing. Only as we move and act in the Holy Spirit are we any kind of threat to him. We are powerless to affect his kingdom outside of the anointing. We can threaten the devil all day, and all night, but if we are not moving in the Spirit, he is not a bit afraid of us."

(Note): On my way to this particular prayer meeting, I had lost a button from the front of my dress. One of the sisters noticed it, found another button that matched, brought me a needle and thread and helped me sew it back on. I was blessed. I hope we all learn to be that kind of blessing. The Bible says that, "...love will cover a multitude of sins" **(1 Pet. 4:8).** *"For it is God who works in you both to will and to do for His good pleasure"* **(Phil. 2:13).**

Let's allow Him to do a great and mighty work. There is a wonderful outpouring at this present time of signs and wonders in the Body of Christ. The love of God let loose in us would be the greatest sign and wonder of them all. Do it, Lord!

—Chapter Thirteen —

Crucified With Christ

If you are faced with a situation where there is accusation, or if you feel that you are treated unjustly or unfairly, stay in the truth and don't **react**. Jesus never **reacted** to anything. He only **acted** under the anointing of the Holy Spirit. If you are feeling angry, refrain from saying anything. Remember Romans, chapter six. The **old man** has been crucified with Christ. Don't allow him to rise up and interfere. What you are feeling in the natural has to die. Your judgment will be wrong. Remember that the Lord knows the intents of the heart, and you don't. Sometimes people do and say things that, in their hearts, they don't mean. In other words, if you have been hurt by someone, it may be through misunderstanding, and not the deliberate intent of that person to hurt you. When you let go of your anger, etc., then the Holy Spirit can open your eyes and show you what **He** sees.

I always try to think like this when these situations occur. I am crucified with Christ, the old man has been rendered dead. If you came upon a dead body laying in the street and you kicked it, what do you think would happen? Nothing, of course, dead people don't **react**! If there was a fault with the other person or people, maybe the Lord will give you a word, and the opportunity to give it; but it will only be when you are free from the situation, and free from your anger. Perhaps He will not give you anything; you may just have to trust Him to deal with it another way or through someone else. Maybe He will use someone you don't even know.

Sometime ago, Cathy, our ex-secretary and a close friend of mine, was put in a situation where she was extremely upset and angry with someone in a meeting. She left the meeting, but one of the women followed her out and persuaded her to come back and, "get it off her chest." She did not want to say anything at the time as she recognized that she certainly was not in the right spirit. Some of the people thought it was good that she should be honest and speak the "truth."

Although the group was well meaning, they did not understand the way of the Holy Spirit. She was right to keep silent, and they should have left it at that. In her anger she couldn't see everything straight and said things that she later regretted. They were not necessary and definitely not helpful to anyone. She was only left with a feeling of condemnation because she lashed out in anger. The Holy Spirit's way will bring life to you or through you, even though it may seem harder at the time to be still and keep silent.

Chapter Fourteen

Taking on False Burdens

God is going to bring a strong and powerful anointing upon the Church. It is what I call the "Lion Anointing." There is coming forth a mighty roar from the Lion of the Tribe of Judah. It will break every chain and shatter every bondage. The roar is beginning in a small way to echo through the Body of Christ. Be prepared for war, for the battle of the ages. Soon Jesus will come to take His position of all authority. We are going to rule and reign with Him. He is making us ready. The Holy Spirit is revealing Jesus, causing those who are dry to be filled with fresh oil, those who are thirsty to be filled with new wine. The faint are receiving a new breath of life. He is restoring His joy so that we may have that strength in the face of the enemy.

God looks on His enemies and laughs the scripture declared in Psalm Two. Why then are we so worried about the devil and his agents? We seem to get under false burdens and false responsibilities so easily. God knows what He is doing, He has everything under control. He is not running around like "a cat on a hot tin roof," trying to juggle the affairs of the Kingdom. We can have confidence and authority, if we learn to operate in the Spirit and stay in the anointing.

I do a fair amount of interceding and praying for ministries and churches. It was such a great relief to me when the Holy Spirit told me that I wasn't called to "stand in the gap" like people kept telling me. What a burden and responsibility that was! I'll tell you a secret that will set you free. Jesus is the **one** who stood in the gap. He is the Intercessor. He is ever living in this capacity and office **(Heb. 7:25).** We are privileged to have a part and share in this ministry, but it is not heavy.

As we yield to the Spirit, He uses us and gives us words of knowledge and discernment and other gifts of the Spirit to enable us to pray according to the will of God. Having the mind of Christ, we can pray effectively **(Phil. 2:5, 1 Cor. 2:16).** When we pray in this way, it **always** comes to pass. God doesn't know how to fail. We just have to do what He's doing. Jesus showed us how. He did not minister to needs, He ministered to the Father. The Father told Him what to say, where to go, and what to do. He did not make His own decisions, He didn't even think His own thoughts about things. He listened to the Father and spoke what He heard from heaven. As previously mentioned, **Jesus didn't make His own judgments** by the seeing of His eyes or the hearing of His ears. It is not complicated. **His yoke is easy, His burden is light (Mt. 11:30).**

Several years ago I was praying with a group of women in Orlando, Florida, where I used to live. Every day we got together and prayed. We did battle against Satan. We even did battle against some of the saints. Of course we thought

God was on our side and we made judgments about things and people out of ignorance. Because we prayed so much and God revealed a lot of things to us, we became rather self-righteous and judgmental. Our prayer meetings became almost an obsession, because we thought that God's Kingdom was somehow dependent upon us and our prayers.

The Lord was very merciful and sent someone with a word of knowledge and a lot of compassion. We were delivered from a spirit of war, which was demonic. Now that may shock you, but we had gotten over into a pride-like place. One of the elders in our church, Gary, prayed over me and said, "Jesus, please show Kathie that **You** are the one who stood in the gap, not her." When that elder spoke those words, it felt like a ton weight had been lifted off my shoulders.

I have never been the same since that day. I had a great revelation. I rested in Jesus's finished work as the Intercessor. He allows me to be used, because He desires me to be blessed. I no longer feel that God's kingdom is not going to make it if I don't pray. I still pray a lot, but now it is easy, because I am no longer striving. I am learning to rest according to Hebrews, chapter four, which is a great revelation to live in. *"There remains therefore a rest for the people of God. For he who has entered His rest has himself also ceased from his works as God did from His"* (**Heb. 4:9-10**).

As I wait on the Lord, He gives me many visions, dreams, words of knowledge and words of wisdom. He also shows me what He is doing in people's lives. He tells me how and what to pray. It is easy, it's not a heavy yoke. I make myself available to the Holy Spirit. He sometimes comes strong with weeping. Sometimes I pray in tongues for several hours, knowing there is a major battle going on in the heavenlies.

But it's not my battle, it's His. I pray until the anointing lifts and I have that sense of victory in my spirit. If the Lord tells me what demonic spirits to pray against, I do so. Sometimes He doesn't tell me. I just know that I am interceding for someone. If He tells me what is going on in that person's life, it's great, but if He doesn't choose to tell me, that's O.K., too.

An old pastor that I once knew told me this, *"Kathie, we are to be like a knife and fork on a table; we are to be available. If God desires to use us, He picks us up, but when He's not particularly using us, we have to learn to be happy, just being with Jesus."* This pastor would just glance at people sometimes, or speak one word, or just touch them, and they would fall down and get delivered instantly. He had a relationship with God. I felt he knew what he was talking about, so I listened. If someone is telling you how to do something, take a look and see if it's working for them. If it isn't, they can only give you information, and not revelation.

False Anointings

I have been to a few intercessors' conferences, and I sometimes feel that old spirit of heaviness coming upon the people. I know what's happening. It's usually a heavy exhortation to "stand in the gap." The spirit of religion loves it. As long as that spirit can make us take on false responsibility, it knows it will get us out of the anointing, and separated from the joy of the Lord. The devil is very clever, we underestimate his ability to manipulate us. If he can get us out of the joy of our salvation, then we have no strength in the Spirit for, *"The joy of the Lord is your strength"* (**Neh. 8:10**).

Occasionally I see prayer warriors operating in a false anointing. They are under a heaviness because Satan has them yoked to a ministry instead of being yoked to Jesus. *"Take my yoke upon you and learn from Me, for I am gentle and lowly in heart, and you will find rest for your souls. For My yoke is easy and My burden is light"* **(Mt. 11:29-30).** The "Lion anointing" is our Heavenly Father's anointing, it is not ours. It is not to be confused with natural aggression. I have met many well-intentioned young people. They want to be warriors, but they are operating in a soulish strength. Because they are aggressive they think they have power in the Spirit. Sometimes they have power, but it is not the Holy Spirit's power. It's a false anointing.

God's way is that we learn to walk **by faith** in the new nature. It is anything but aggressive in the natural. That's not to say we are supposed to have a wimpy kind of personality. I have met men and women with strong personalities who are not dominating and controlling. They are pleasant and gracious. The "Lion anointing" is going to come strongest upon those who walk in the "Lamb nature."

The power of the Holy Spirit is His power exclusively, not ours. We are just the vessels, and any kind of vessel will do. Black, white, yellow, big, small, thin, fat, smart, or not so smart. We tend to look at the vessel rather than the treasure. If the vessel does not meet with our approval, then we judge it to be unworthy. The pharisee spirit always wants to influence us to make people "qualify" in some way before God can use them.

Since we have lived here in America, we have noticed the separation between black and white people. There are black churches, white churches, Hispanic churches, etc. Although some of this is understandable, because of language, culture, or style of music, much of it is just blind prejudice.

We are going to see more multi-racial churches arising with the power of God. These are the ones that are going to prosper and increase. *"For He Himself is our peace, who has made both one, and has broken down the middle wall of separation..."* (**Eph. 2:14**). *"After these things I looked, and behold, a great multitude which none could number, **of all nations, tribes, peoples, and tongues,** standing before the throne and before the Lamb, **clothed with white robes,** with palm branches in their hands, and crying out with a **loud voice,** saying, 'Salvation to our God who sits on the throne, and to the Lamb!'"* (**Rev. 7:9-10**).

We have also noticed a separation between adults and children in America. Churches that continually separate the children from the adults, prejudge children's spiritual ability. Some of the most awesome miracles and healings we have seen, have come through the Lord using yielded, believing little vessels, whom we call children. Many of them in my husband's meetings have been taken into heaven in their spirits. They have seen angels. They have been used powerfully by God in operating in the gifts of the Spirit. Many people have received healings and miracles through the laying on of grubby little hands.

The Lamb Nature

We all can quote the scripture, *"...not by might nor by power, but by My Spirit, says the Lord of hosts"* (**Zech. 4:6**). But we still continue to try and find something in ourselves to offer to God. He doesn't want it. The things, however good they may appear, that are initiated from the human spirit (old man), are useless and worthless. They cannot produce life. *"...We have this treasure [life of God] in earthen vessels...*

[fleshly bodies] " **(2 Cor. 4:7).** It is the treasure (Holy Spirit) that produces life. Look at it this way. If you went outside into your yard and planted in the ground an old tin can, you can do what you will. Tend it, feed it, water it or fertilize it faithfully, it will never produce anything. That is like the works of our flesh. On the outside it can look good, have an attractive label, but in terms of the eternal, it is dead and will produce nothing.

Allow the "Lamb nature" to be manifested in you. It's the opposite to the natural (wolf) nature. The Lord will pour His Spirit upon us and fill us with His anointing if we walk as He shows us. Let us leave the ways of the flesh. All judgments that we make from our own flesh are made out of pride, as if we knew the heart of another. Let's leave the old pharisaical ways and go on in the Spirit. Let's allow God's love, compassion, grace and loving kindness to flow like a river through us, His beloved church.

If you feel that you have come under the judgments of the Pharisee spirit, cut it off from your life in the Name of Jesus. If in turn, you feel that you have made judgments out of your own heart, release that person, or church, or ministry and ask the Lord to forgive you. Humble yourself under His mighty hand and remember that it is only because of His grace that any one of us is able to stand.

Included are some insights and testimonies that will bless you, if you take a few more minutes to read them. I hope you will.

Kathie Walters

GOD'S POLICEMAN
Contributed by WG. CMDR. MICK OXLEY

(Mick is from Great Britain. He and his wife, Betty, have a ministry in Florida and God uses them to minister to many people who have been in bondage to various cults.)

When I look back over the past few years, it is amazing to see how the Lord, in His infinite grace, has delivered me from a critical and judgmental spirit. I had very strong convictions of how I felt others [especially those involved in ministry] should believe and live. Everyone was measured by my standards, not necessarily God's Word. I felt a need to constantly tell Jesus how He should correct other people. Needless to say, I became very miserable and managed to cut myself off from the voice of the Lord by my negative attitude. My wife, Betty, and I lost our love of the brethren [at least those who did not agree with us] and we finally ended up almost hating those we believed to be wrong. We even rejoiced in their downfall. As friends prayed for us, the Lord began to break through the darkness we found ourselves in. Over a period of time, we began to hear what the Lord was saying to us about tolerance.

One of the meanings of the word "tolerance" is forbearing. *"With all lowliness and gentleness, with longsuffering, bearing with one another in love, endeavoring to keep the unity of the Spirit in the bond of peace"* **(Eph. 4:2-3).** I began to realize that as I judged and criticized others, I was actually in rebellion toward God.

When Aaron and Miriam confronted and challenged Moses about his marriage to an Ethiopian woman, God regarded it as rebellion and Miriam immediately became leprous (unclean).

When we began to pray for those we had found fault with, God was able to work in us and change our attitude and perception of them. We began to see through the eyes of Jesus. Then we had a much clearer vision. Negative thought patterns like to hang around the corners of our minds. They are like cobwebs in a corner of a room. You have to make an effort to sweep them clean. A thought pattern is sometimes hard to break. Our only desire now in our ministry is to glorify Jesus, and lift up the saints. The exposing done now in our ministry is to set free those in bondage to false religion."

After serving many years as personal air crew to prime ministers, royalty and other dignitaries, Mick Oxley retired from the Royal Air Force as Wing Commander in 1977. The same year, he and his wife, Betty, moved to Florida. Mick had spent many years seeking for truth in many false religions. He became a Master Mason in the English Constitution. Finally, he found THE TRUTH and he and his family became enthusiastic Christians. Mick is the founder of "In His Grip Ministries," Rt. 1, Box 257E, Paradise Shore Rd., Crescent City, Florida 32112.

POWER OF HIS LOVE
Contributed by ROSE WEINER

(Rose and her husband, Bob, live in Gainesville, Florida. Their ministry reaches into every nation. Bob and Rose have a special burden for the young people in Russia, China, and the U.S.A. to be reached with the Gospel, and then to be trained to minister to their own people. The Weiners motivate thousands of young people all over the world to fulfill their calling and destiny).

"The person who has My commandments and keeps them is the one who [really] loves Me, and whoever [really] loves Me, will be loved by My Father and I [too] will love him and will show [reveal, manifest] Myself to him. I will let Myself be clearly seen by him and will make Myself real to him" **(Jn. 14:21, Amplified Bible).**

Jesus demonstrated the depths of love and forgiveness the church must show. We are meant to be an exhibit, for the world to see; God's showcase, to demonstrate His power. Not only in miracles of healing, but by His manifested life in us. The power of His forgiveness, His love, and mercy, are only going to be seen by the world as it observes the church. The world has not seen too much of this. That doesn't mean it is not there. The media is not so quick to relay reports of us all loving and forgiving each other, as it is to tell of our failures. But, in our own hearts we know what we are allowing the Holy Spirit to demonstrate.

Saul of Tarsus (later Paul) persecuted and imprisoned great numbers of Christians. Then God saved him and filled him with His HOLY Spirit; not only saved and filled, but entrusted to Paul the mysteries of the New Covenant. God anointed him to teach the church the doctrines of redemption. Paul was given revelations of the spiritual realms and even heaven. Did you ever realize how hard it must have been for some of those New Testament saints to receive from Paul? To receive from him they had to love him. God was giving this Paul, who had persecuted them mercilessly, revelation that they had not had.

Remember Jesus said, *"...And he who loves me will be loved by My Father, and I will love him and manifest Myself to him"* **(Jn. 14:21).**

If the church had not received and been prepared to love and forgive Paul, they would not have been able to receive what God wanted to give them. Their eyes would have been blinded, and the things of the Spirit would have been foolishness to them. Because of the critical nature of many spiritual self-appointed policemen, the moving of the Spirit becomes foolishness in their eyes and they mock and make light of the ministries of people who allow the demonstration of God's power in their meetings and their lives. Maybe it would befit them to learn to love the Body of Christ more, and then they would be able to see better the hidden things of God, and receive a stronger anointing upon their own lives and ministries.

GOD'S TIME
Contributed by PASTOR BILL GROGAN

(Bill and his wife, Carol, are originally from Liverpool, England, where he both started and pastored a church. He also ministered widely in the U.S. and Canada. In 1987 He and his family moved to the U.S.A. to take the position of seminar director at a ministry in Northern Minnesota. He is presently pastoring The Country Church, P.O. Box 19, Goodland, Minnesota 55742. (218) 492-4248

In the scriptures we are admonished about making judgments and appraisals according to the flesh or by mere natural observance and understanding. *"Therefore do not go on passing judgment before the time, but wait until the Lord comes who will both bring to light the things hidden in the darkness and disclose the motives of men's hearts; and then each man's praise will come to him from God"* **(1 Cor. 4:5).**

We are warned in this scripture about making judgments before the appropriate **time.** We can so often make hasty judgments and form opinions without giving sufficient **time** to prove the veracity of a word spoken or an action taken. There are a number of examples in the scriptures where people claimed to have been spoken to by God or spoke for God and, at first, it appeared as though they may have been mistaken, but ultimately **time** proved them to be correct.

Joseph was given two dreams; that one day all his family would bow down before him and he would be in a position of great authority. These dreams caused resentment and jealousy among his brothers and consternation from his parents. For about fourteen years after these dreams were given it seemed that everything in Joseph's life was going in the opposite direction and that the dreams were the proud, false imaginations of a youthful heart. God, however, had His own timetable of events and Joseph's whole family did eventually bow down before him. Joseph was used to rescue and preserve his people through a time of the great famine. Let us learn to wait, and not be hasty in our assessments and judgments of events, situations and prophecies. **Time** will tell.

RIGHT JUDGMENT VERSUS OPINIONS
Contributed by RENEE PLOUFF

(Renee and her husband, Michael, have four children. They live near Stone Mountain, Georgia. Renee's heart is to encourage the Body of Christ to become the beloved Bride and to submit to the beautifying work of the Holy Spirit.)

To offer our opinions and insist on giving forth our judgments about God's people should not be on our agenda. A disciple is never above his Master **(Mt. 10:24).** To imagine that our thoughts are superior to those of our Lord is ludicrous, but when we give our own ideas and opinions, we exalt ourselves above our Master. When we set ourselves above our Master, we set ourselves in direct opposition to the Spirit of God, and we put ourselves into a most dangerous position, because we are asserting our own standards. *"There is only one Lawgiver and Judge, the One who is able to save and to destroy; but who are you who judge your neighbor?"* (**Jas. 4:12**). When we judge our neighbor, we remove ourselves from the righteousness provided through the perfect work of the cross and we demand that God judge us according to our own righteousness. By making our own judgments we are proclaiming before God that we believe that our judgments have merit of their own, and we have no need of His righteousness. We are declaring that His offer of pardon for our past sins and the continuing cleansing work of the shed blood of His Son on the cross is not necessary in our case.

It is an easy thing to turn away from something that you despise. Pray that the Holy Spirit would cause you to recognize judgments that spring from your own mind and soul. Ask Him to reveal the vanity of such thoughts and to bring a loathing that would accompany every carnal judgment and opinion. He longs to liberate us from everything that controls and condemns us. He is longing to cleanse us. Our beautification as the Bride of Christ is His sole responsibility, for *"He [and He alone] is able to present us faultless before the Presence of His glory with exceeding joy"* (**Jude 24**). He longs to do this work of preparation in us. The work He has begun, He will finish (**Phil. 1:6**). If we will pray for the revelation of the Holy Spirit and repent when He brings the ugliness of our own judgments and opinions to light, we will know freedom like we have never imagined. And we will know the joy of

His continuing presence in a way that will eclipse our past knowledge of God. We will have life abundantly as promised **(Jn. 10:10).**

The life of Jesus is glorious. It is perfect and beautiful. What an exhilarating feeling to walk in Christ! Not having any righteousness of our own. *"But of Him are you in Christ Jesus, who of God is made unto us Wisdom, Righteousness, Sanctification and Redemption"* **(1 Cor. 1:30).** It is God's desire that we should operate in the mind of Christ, and allow His heart to be revealed in us. It is a glorious and exciting revelation, to know what God thinks about things. It is a great relief to know that we are not responsible to make judgments about anything. He will make the judgments, our place is to listen, agree with Him, act and speak accordingly.

We must forsake all things that war against His life in us. We have been called into His wondrous light. *"...In Him there is **no** darkness at all"* **(1 Jn. 1:5).** We must not live in the darkness of our own judgments and opinions. To do so is to spurn the love of the Son of God. He is so lovely. He longingly looks to you and me. We are the apple of His eye **(Zech. 2:8).**

Books Available Through
Good News Fellowship Ministries

By Kathie Walters

Living in the Supernatural — Kathie believes that the supernatural realm, angels, miracles, and signs and wonders are the inheritance of every believer and should be a part of our life. She tells how to embrace and enter into our inheritance.

Parenting — By the Spirit — Kathie shows how to raise your children by being led of the Spirit. She believes that we are to raise anointed and radical kids who serve the Lord from a very young age.

By David Walters

Kids in Combat — David shows how to train children and teens in spiritual power and bring them into the anointing. (Parents, teachers and children/youth pastors)

Equipping the Younger Saints — Teaching children and youth the Baptism of the Holy Spirit and spiritual gifts. (Parents, teachers, youth/children's pastors)

Armor of God — Children's illustrated Bible study on Ephesians 6:10-18. (Ages 6-14 years)

Fruit of the Spirit — Children's illustrated Bible study on spiritual fruit in our lives. (Ages 7-14 years)

Fact or Fantasy — Children's illustrated Bible study on Christian apologetics. How to defend your faith. (Ages 8-15)

Being a Christian — Children's illustrated Bible study on what it really means to be a Christian. (Ages 7-14 years)

By Roberts Liardon

I Saw Heaven — Roberts tells of his experience as a young boy when God visited him in a special way and took him into heaven. God revealed to Roberts the call on his life. (Child-adult)

Call or write for further information and order forms to:

GOOD NEWS FELLOWSHIP MINISTRIES
RT. 28, BOX 95D, SLEEPY CREEK ROAD
MACON, GEORGIA 31210
PHONE (912) 757-8071
FAX (912) 757-0136

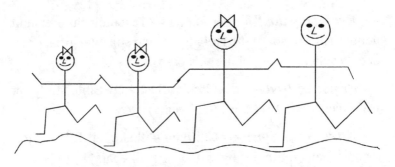

About the Walters Family

David and Kathie Walters are originally from England. They have lived and ministered in the United States for eighteen years. They presently reside in Macon, Georgia.

David has a burden for what he terms church-wise kids and teens — those who have been brought up in the church and have a head knowledge of the things of God. His desire is for the young people to have a dynamic experience of God for themselves. His "Raising Anointed Children and Youth" seminars are for children/teens, youth pastors and parents. He also holds revival meetings for churches and includes the children and teens in the miracle ministry of the Holy Spirit. David ministers at many National Conferences in the U.S. and overseas.

Kathie ministers alongside David and also has a desire to see God's women come forth in all their anointings and giftings. She believes that the realm of the Spirit, the supernatural power of God, heaven and angels are our inheritance and are meant to be a normal part of our lives and the life of the church. She also believes in Spirit-led parenting.

Faith, 17, and Lisa, 14, are anointed and already moving in their giftings. They both love to travel. Faith ministers in dance and prophecy and Lisa sings and ministers the gifts of the Spirit.